Owen

by Iain Gray

GW00657507

Lang**Syne**
PUBLISHING
WRITING *to* REMEMBER

Lang**Syne**

PUBLISHING

WRITING *to* REMEMBER

79 Main Street, Newtongrange,
Midlothian EH22 4NA
Tel: 0131 344 0414   Fax: 0845 075 6085
E-mail: info@lang-syne.co.uk
www.langsyneshop.co.uk

Design by Dorothy Meikle
Printed by Printwell Ltd
© Lang Syne Publishers Ltd 2016

ISBN 978-1-85217-538-2

Owen

MOTTO:
Honesty is the best policy.

CREST:
The head of an eagle
(and)
A lion rampant.

NAME variations include:
Owens
Owenson
Owenby

Chapter one:

The origins of popular surnames

by George Forbes and Iain Gray

***If you don't know where you came from, you won't know where you're going** is a frequently quoted observation and one that has a particular resonance today when there has been a marked upsurge in interest in genealogy, with increasing numbers of people curious to trace their family roots.*

Main sources for genealogical research include census returns and official records of births, marriages and deaths – and the key to unlocking the detail they contain is obviously a family surname, one that has been 'inherited' and passed from generation to generation.

No matter our station in life, we all have a surname – but it was not until about the middle of the fourteenth century that the practice of being identified by a particular surname became commonly established throughout the British Isles.

Previous to this, it was normal for a person to be identified through the use of only a forename.

But as population gradually increased and there were many more people with the same forename, surnames were adopted to distinguish one person, or community, from another.

Many common English surnames are patronymic in origin, meaning they stem from the forename of one's father – with 'Johnson,' for example, indicating 'son of John.'

It was the Normans, in the wake of their eleventh century conquest of Anglo-Saxon England, a pivotal moment in the nation's history, who first brought surnames into usage – although it was a gradual process.

For the Normans, these were names initially based on the title of their estates, local villages and chateaux in France to distinguish and identify these landholdings.

Such grand descriptions also helped enhance the prestige of these warlords and generally glorify their lofty positions high above the humble serfs slaving away below in the pecking order who had only single names, often with Biblical connotations as in Pierre and Jacques.

The only descriptive distinctions among the peasantry concerned their occupations, like 'Pierre the swineherd' or 'Jacques the ferryman.'

Roots of surnames that came into usage in England not only included Norman-French, but also Old French, Old Norse, Old English, Middle English, German, Latin, Greek, Hebrew and the Gaelic languages of the Celts.

The Normans themselves were originally Vikings, or 'Northmen', who raided, colonised and eventually settled down around the French coastline.

The had sailed up the Seine in their longboats in 900AD under their ferocious leader Rollo and ruled the roost in north eastern France before sailing over to conquer England in 1066 under Duke William of Normandy – better known to posterity as William the Conqueror, or King William I of England.

Granted lands in the newly-conquered England, some of their descendants later acquired territories in Wales, Scotland and Ireland – taking not only their own surnames, but also the practice of adopting a surname, with them.

But it was in England where Norman rule and custom first impacted, particularly in relation to the adoption of surnames.

This is reflected in the famous *Domesday Book*, a massive survey of much of England and Wales, ordered by William I, to determine who owned what, what it was worth and therefore how much they were liable to pay in taxes to the voracious Royal Exchequer.

Completed in 1086 and now held in the National Archives in Kew, London, 'Domesday' was an Old English word meaning 'Day of Judgement.'

This was because, in the words of one contemporary chronicler, "its decisions, like those of the Last Judgement, are unalterable."

It had been a requirement of all those English landholders – from the richest to the poorest – that they identify themselves for the purposes of the survey and for future reference by means of a surname.

This is why the *Domesday Book*, although written in Latin as was the practice for several centuries with both civic and ecclesiastical records, is an invaluable source for the early appearance of a wide range of English surnames.

Several of these names were coined in connection with occupations.

These include Baker and Smith, while Cooks, Chamberlains, Constables and Porters were to be found carrying out duties in large medieval households.

The church's influence can be found in names such as Bishop, Friar and Monk while the popular name of Bennett derives from the late fifth to mid-sixth century Saint Benedict, founder of the Benedictine order of monks.

The early medical profession is represented by Barber, while businessmen produced names that include Merchant and Sellers.

Down at the village watermill, the names that cropped up included Millar/Miller, Walker and Fuller, while other self-explanatory trades included Cooper, Tailor, Mason and Wright.

Even the scenery was utilised as in Moor, Hill, Wood and Forrest – while the hunt and the chase supplied names that include Hunter, Falconer, Fowler and Fox.

Colours are also a source of popular surnames, as in Black, Brown, Gray/Grey, Green and White, and would have denoted the colour of the clothing the person habitually wore or, apart from the obvious exception of 'Green', one's hair colouring or even complexion.

The surname Red developed into Reid, while

Blue was rare and no-one wanted to be associated with yellow.

Rather self-important individuals took surnames that include Goodman and Wiseman, while physical attributes crept into surnames such as Small and Little.

Many families proudly boast the heraldic device known as a Coat of Arms, as featured on our front cover.

The central motif of the Coat of Arms would originally have been what was borne on the shield of a warrior to distinguish himself from others on the battlefield.

Not featured on the Coat of Arms, but high-lighted on page three, is the family motto and related crest – with the latter frequently different from the central motif.

Adding further variety to the rich cultural heritage that is represented by surnames is the appearance in recent times in lists of the 100 most common names found in England of ones that include Khan, Patel and Singh – names that have proud roots in the vast sub-continent of India.

Echoes of a far distant past can still be found in our surnames and they can be borne with pride in commemoration of our forebears.

Chapter two:

Ancient Britons

Although ranked at 88th in some lists of the 100 most common surnames in England, 'Owen' is nevertheless particularly identified with Wales.

Derived from the Welsh personal name 'Owen' or 'Owain' and whose Old Welsh forms were 'Ouein' and 'Ouen', it stems from the Latin 'Eugenius' which, in turn, derives from the Greek 'Eugenios' – indicating 'of noble birth.'

Although, in common with many other surnames, it was popularised in the wake of the Norman Conquest of 1066, some of those who would later adopt it pre-date the arrival on British shores of invaders such as the Romans, Vikings, Anglo-Saxons and Normans.

This means that flowing through the veins of many bearers of the Owen name today is the blood of the ancient Britons.

Of Celtic pedigree, these early inhabitants of the British Isles were settled for centuries from a line south of the River Forth in Scotland all the way down to the south coast of England and with a particular presence in Wales.

Speaking a Celtic language known as Brythonic, they boasted a glorious culture that flourished even after the Roman invasion of Britain in 43 AD and the subsequent consolidation of Roman power by about 84 AD.

With many of the original Britons absorbing aspects of Roman culture, they became 'Romano-British' – while still retaining their own proud Celtic heritage.

Following the withdrawal of the last Roman legions from Britain in 406, what is now modern-day Wales, or *Cymru*, fragmented into a number of independent kingdoms – with the most powerful king being regarded as overall ruler.

Recognised as King of the Britons, he had to battle with not only internal rivals but also the depredations of the wild sea rovers known as the Vikings, or Northmen.

There were also the Anglo-Saxons to contend with – as those Germanic tribes who invaded and settled in the south and east of the island of Britain from about the early fifth century were known.

They were composed of the Jutes, from the

area of the Jutland Peninsula in modern Denmark, the Saxons from Lower Saxony, in modern Germany and the Angles from the Angeln area of Germany.

It was the Angles who gave the name 'Engla land', or 'Aengla land' – better known as 'England.'

The Anglo-Saxons held sway in what became England from approximately 550 to 1066, with the main kingdoms those of Sussex, Wessex, Northumbria, Mercia, Kent, East Anglia and Essex.

Whoever controlled the most powerful of these kingdoms was tacitly recognised as overall 'king' – one of the most noted being Alfred the Great, King of Wessex from 871 to 899.

The Anglo-Saxons, meanwhile, had usurped the power of the indigenous Britons, such as those found in Wales, and who referred to them as 'Saeson' or 'Saxones.'

It is from this that the Scottish Gaelic term for 'English people' of 'Sasannach' derives, the Irish Gaelic 'Sasanach' and the Welsh 'Saeson.'

The death knell of Anglo-Saxon supremacy and also what remained of Welsh independence was sounded with the Norman Conquest and the defeat of Harold II, the last of the Anglo-Saxon monarchs, at the battle of Hastings.

Within an astonishingly short space of time, Norman manners, customs and law were imposed on England – laying the basis for what subsequently became established 'English' custom and practice.

In 1282, by which time most of Wales had come under Anglo-Norman rule, final rebellion against this was crushed by England's Edward I, and it is from this date that the heir apparent to the British throne has borne the title of Prince of Wales.

An abortive rebellion was led in the early fifteenth century by the freedom fighter Owain Glyndŵr, while in the following century, under Henry VIII, Wales was 'incorporated' into the English kingdom; in 1707, in common with Scotland, Wales became part of the United Kingdom.

Flourishing not only in their original heartland of Wales but also throughout the British Isles, bearers of the Owen name feature prominently in the historical record.

Responsible for rescuing his homeland's folklore and traditions from obscurity, Elias Owen was the distinguished Welsh cleric and antiquarian born in the small village of Llandysilio, Montgomeryshire in 1833.

The son of a farmer who, through his two

marriages fathered no fewer than fifteen children, he graduated from Trinity College, Dublin in 1871 after earlier studying at the Oxford Diocesan Training College for Schoolmasters.

Working for a time as headmaster of a school from about the mid-1850s until 1871, at Llanllechid, near Bangor, his imagination was fired by the rich wealth of antiquities that the area boasted.

Along with local vicar John Evans, he explored the local mountains and meticulously mapped what had been a Roman encampment on the slopes of Foel-fras.

Later creating a detailed map of his parish, this was published in *Archaeologia Cambrensis – Archaeology of Wales*.

Curate from 1871 until 1875 at St Gwynnog's Church, Llanwnog and also working as a schools' inspector, he travelled widely and took the opportunity to get elderly inhabitants he met to relate their colourful tales of ancient traditions and superstitions.

These tales were collected and published in 1896 as *Welsh Folk-Lore: A Collection of the Folk-Tales and Legends of North Wales*; a Fellow of the Society of Antiquaries of London, he died in 1899.

Chapter three:

Discovery and invention

One particularly intrepid bearer of the Owen name was the British Royal Naval explorer Vice Admiral William Owen, who made a number of noted voyages of discovery.

Born in Manchester in 1774, the illegitimate son of a Captain William Owen, he was orphaned when aged four and taken along with his older brother into the care of a family friend, Rear Admiral Sir Thomas Rich.

Taking to the high seas as a midshipman when aged 13 aboard Rich's vessel HMS *Culloden*, he was commissioned as a lieutenant in 1797 and, six years later, given command of the brig *Seaflower*, operating in the East Indies.

Exploring the Maldive Islands in 1806 he also discovered the channel between the islands of Sipora and Siberut, off the west coast of Sumatra, subsequently named Seaflower Channel.

Fighting the Dutch in the East Indies two years later, in 1815 and 1816 he was in the waters of North America, surveying the upper Canadian Great

Lakes, and naming an inlet on Georgian Bay Owen's Sound in honour of his brother and fellow naval commander Admiral William Owen.

Operating from the sloop *Leven* and the brig *Barratcouta*, between 1821 and 1826 he mapped the entire coast of east Africa from the Cape to the Horn of Africa, having covered some 30,000 miles of coastline and battling against tropical diseases that killed more than half of his original crews.

Later settling in St John, New Brunswick, he died in 1857.

On the bloody field of battle, Wilfred Owen was the soldier and acclaimed poet of the First World War born of mixed English and Welsh roots in 1893 near Oswestry, Shropshire.

Working for a time in France as a private tutor of English and French, on the outbreak of war he enlisted in the Artists' Rifles Officers Training Corps, being commissioned as a second lieutenant in June of 1916.

His experiences of the hell of the Western Front were traumatic – being blown into the air by a trench mortar and spending at least two days lying out in the open next to the remains of a fellow officer.

Diagnosed as suffering from neurasthenia, or

shell-shock, he was sent for treatment to Craiglockhart War Hospital, Edinburgh and it was here that he met fellow poet Siegfried Sassoon.

Returning to the frontline in August of 1918, he penned a number of memorable poems on the horrors of the conflict that most notably include *Anthem for Doomed Youth*, *Dulce et Decorum Est*, *Insensibility*, *Strange Meeting* and *Futility*.

He was killed in action in November of 1918 – only a week before the signing of the Armistice that ended the conflict.

Nearly 70 years later, in November of 1985, he was one of the 16 Great War poets commemorated on a stone unveiled in Westminster Abbey's Poet's Corner.

The moving inscription on the stone: "My subject is war and the pity of war. The Poetry is in the pity", is taken from his own preface to his poems.

While Wilfred Owen wrote about the horrors of war, Evelyn Owen is famous for having invented the deadly instrument of war known as the Owen Submachine Gun.

Born in 1915 in Wollongong, New South Wales, he managed to overcome bureaucratic and what now appear as ludicrous objections to his invention on the grounds that it was thought, in common with the Thompson Submachine Gun, to be the weapon of American gangsters, rather than soldiers.

Eventually patenting the gun in 1943, it quickly became a popular weapon of choice for soldiers – proving almost impossible to jam even after being immersed in water, mud and sand.

Used extensively throughout the remainder of the Second World War, including against the Japanese in the jungles of New Guinea, it was also used to great effect after his death in 1949 in the Korean and Vietnam wars.

From warfare to the more constructive pursuit of social reform, Robert Owen was the great Welsh social reformer born in Newtown, Montgomeryshire in 1771.

The son of an ironmonger and saddler and the sixth of seven children, he became the manager of a cotton mill in Manchester when aged 21.

Infused with ideas to better the lives of mill workers through social reform, he met like-minded people through his membership of the Manchester Literary and Philosophical Society, later becoming a member of the Manchester Board of Health.

Visiting Scotland in 1799, he met and married

Caroline Dale, daughter of the New Lanark mill proprietor and fellow social reformer David Dale.

Along with a number of business partners, he bought the New Lanark concern – which was powered by water provided by the spectacular Falls of Clyde – and became part-owner and manager in 1810.

Taking a paternalistic concern over the welfare of his workforce, Owen established the 'model village' of New Lanark – a major tourist attraction today – providing homes, schooling and the forerunner of what would later become shops and stores known as 'co-operatives.'

He died in 1858, while three of his sons subsequently went on to stamp their own mark on the historical record.

Born in 1801, Robert Dale Owen immigrated to the United States where, after entering politics, he was instrumental in the introduction of pioneering legislation that included the adoption of common free schools in his state of Indiana.

He died in 1877 while his brother David Dale Owen, born in 1807 became a noted geologist in the United States; he died in 1860, while his younger brother Richard Dale Owen, born in 1810 and who died in 1890, was a noted professor of science at Nashville University.

Bearers of the Owen name have also distinguished themselves in the often cut-throat world of mainstream politics.

Born in 1938 to Welsh parents in Plympton, Devon, David Owen, more properly known as Dr David Owen, is the British politician and medical doctor who was elected Labour Member of Parliament (MP) for the constituency of Plymouth Sutton in 1966 and later as MP for Plymouth Devonport.

His rise through the ranks of government was rapid.

Serving from 1977 to 1979 as Foreign Secretary – at the time the youngest person in more than forty years to have held the post – his disillusionment with what he perceived as a dangerous leftwards swing of the Labour Party led him in 1981 to become one of the "Gang of Four" who founded the Social Democratic Party (SDP).

This was along with fellow Labour moderates Roy Jenkins, Shirley Williams and William Rodgers, and he led the party from 1983 until 1987 before it merged with the Liberal Party to form today's Liberal Democrat Party.

Appointed European co-chairman of the Conference for the Former Yugoslavia in 1992 by Conservative Prime Minister John Major and serving for a time in this post, he is still a prominent spokesman on international affairs and nuclear proliferation.

One particularly intriguing bearer of the proud name of Owen was the American physician and literary 'sleuth' Dr Orville Ward Owen, who subscribed to a complex theory that some of the works of the great English playwright and dramatist William Shakespeare had in fact been written by other authors.

Prominent among these supposed authors was the late sixteenth to early seventeenth century philosopher and writer Sir Francis Bacon – and this gave rise to what is known as the Baconian Theory of Shakespearian authorship and first published in Owen's 1893 to 1895 multi-volume work *Sir Francis Bacon's Cipher Story*.

Claiming he had discovered hidden messages in the works of Bacon and works attributed to Shakespeare, Owen said he had 'proved' this through his invention of a device known as the 'cipher wheel.'

This elaborate 'decoding' device involved a

long strip of canvas on which were printed the works of Shakespeare, Bacon and others. A primitive form of modern computer, the cipher wheel was attached to the canvas and, when turned, highlighted key words and phrases and correlations.

Increasingly obsessed with his theory, Owen died in 1924 in a state described by contemporaries as 'a bedridden and almost penniless invalid' – while among his final words was an admonition to others not to follow in his path.

Despite this warning, however, others have continued to pursue his theory.

These include the American 'disciple' of Owen, Virginia Fellows, who spent a lifetime writing her best-selling *The Shakespeare Code*, published in 2006 shortly after her death.

Chapter four:

On the world stage

Born in London in 1914, William John Rowbotham was the English actor better known as Bill Owen.

Best known for his role of 'Compo' Simmonite in the popular television sitcom *Last of the Summer Wine*, his other television credits include *Whatever Happened to the Likely Lads* and *Taxi!*

Also a songwriter, composing the 1968 Cliff Richard hit *Marianne*, his big screen credits include the 1953 *A Day to Remember*, the 1958 *Carve Her Name with Pride*, the 1966 *Georgy Girl* and, from 1975, *The Comeback*.

The recipient of an MBE for his services to acting, he died in 1999, while he was the father of the actor **Tom Owen**.

Born in Brighton in 1949, it was following the death of his father that he took on the television role of his son Tom in *Last of the Summer Wine*, while other television credits include *Z-Cars*, *Upstairs, Downstairs*, *The Onedin Line* and *Minder*.

Born in Coventry in 1964, **Clive Owen** is the English actor of stage, television and film who won a

BAFTA Award, Golden Globe Award and Academy Award nomination for Best Supporting Actor for his role in the 2004 film *Closer*.

Other major film credits include the 1997 *Croupier*, the 2001 *Gosford Park*, the 2002 *The Bourne Identity* and the 2012 *Blood Ties*.

A Welsh actor and television producer, Jonathan Tudor Owen, better known as **Jonny Owen**, was born in 1971 in Merthyr Tydfil.

A Welsh Boys Club Boxing champion when he was a teenager, he has since had roles in television series that include *Shameless*, the *Doctor Who* spin-off *Torchwood*, *Wedding Belles* and *Murphy's Law*, while he writes and produces for ITV Wales.

Also a commentator, presenter and writer on football and rugby, his big screen credits include the 2013 *Svengali*.

Also in the original Owen heartland of Wales, **Kai Owen**, born in 1975 in Llanrwst, is the actor of stage and screen known for his portrayal of Rhys Williams in *Torchwood*, while other television credits include the medical drama *Casualty*, *Being Human* and *Waterloo Road*.

Born in London in 1966, **Lloyd Owen** is the British actor who, after training at the National Youth

Theatre and the Royal Academy of Dramatic Arts,
London has gone on to gain television credits that
include *The Young Indiana Jones Chronicles* and
Monarch of the Glen, while big screen credits include
the 2006 *Miss Potter* and the 2011 *Apollo 18*.

Born in London in 1972, David Sutton is the
English actor, television presenter and singer better
known as **Sid Owen**, known for his role from 1988
to 2012 as Ricky Butcher in the television soap
EastEnders, while he was also a contestant in the
2005 *I'm a Celebrity, Get Me Out of Here* and in the
2012 series of *Strictly Come Dancing*.

Behind the camera lens, **Cliff Owen**, born in
1919 and who died in 1993, was the British television
and film director whose credits include the 1963 *The
Wrong Arm of the Law*, starring Peter Sellers, the
1966 *That Riviera Touch*, starring the comedy duo
Morecambe and Wise, the 1973 *No Sex Please, We're
British* and, from 1976, *The Bawdy Adventures of
Tom Jones*.

Bearers of the Owen name have also excelled
in the highly competitive world of sport.

On the fields of European football, **Michael
Owen**, born in Chester in 1979, is the English striker
who, in addition to playing for the England national

team from 1998 to 2008, earning 89 caps, has also played for teams that include Liverpool, Real Madrid, Newcastle United, Manchester United and Stoke City.

First playing for the England team in 1998, he was the nation's youngest player and youngest goal-scorer at the time.

Winner of the English Premier League Golden Boot Award and awarded the PFA (Professional Footballers Association) Young Player of the Year Award in 1997, he was also the runner-up to French footballer Zinedine Zidane in the World Player of the Year Award.

Born in Chester in 1971, **Gareth Owen** is the Welsh midfielder who, in addition to playing in the Wales Under-21 team and its B team, has played for clubs that include Wrexham, Doncaster Rovers and Rhyl.

His namesake, **Gareth Owen**, born in 1982 in Cheadle, is the English-born Welsh former defender who, in addition to playing for the Wales Under-19 team, also played for clubs that include Stoke City, Oldham Athletic, Stockport County and Port Vale.

In the rough and tumble that is the game of rugby, Richard Morgan Owens, better known as

Dicky Owen, was the player recognised as having been one of Wales' greatest ever scrum-halfs.

Born in 1876, he won 35 caps playing for his nation between 1901 and 1912, while he played club rugby for Swansea; retiring from the game in 1913 and becoming a publican, he tragically took his own life in 1932.

From rugby to the boxing ring, John Owens, born in 1956 in Merthyr Tydfil and who fought under the name of **Johnny Owen**, was the Welsh boxer who held the Bantamweight Championship titles of Great Britain and Europe and was the first Welsh holder of the Bantamweight Championship of the Commonwealth.

Nicknamed the "Merthyr Matchstick" and the "Bionic Bantam" because of his slight physique, he died in November of 1980 after sustaining injuries to his brain in a bout with the Mexican boxer Lupe Pintor – while it later transpired that the boxer had a particularly delicate skull.

A memorial to him was unveiled in Merthyr Tydfil in 2000 and, at the request of his family, the unveiling was performed by Lupe Pintor.

On the golf course, **Greg Owen**, born in 1972 in Mansfield, Nottinghamshire is the English professional golfer who, at the Open Championship in 2001 became the sixth golfer in the history of the competition to score an albatross – double eagle – on the par-5 11th hole at Royal Lytham.

In the highly cerebral world of chess, **John Owen**, born in 1827, was the English vicar and amateur player who devised the chess opening move now named in his honour as Owen's Defence; he died in 1901.

No account of sporting bearers of the Owen name could perhaps be complete without a reference to one of their famous namesakes of the name Owens.

This was the great African-American athlete sprinter **Jesse Owens**.

Famed as the most successful athlete of the 1936 Olympics in Berlin, he won no fewer than four gold medals – in the 100-metres, 200-metres, long jump and as a member of the U.S. 4x400-metres relay team.

This was to the considerable annoyance of the German Führer Adolf Hitler, who had hoped the games would showcase what he and fellow Nazis perceived as 'Aryan racial superiority.'

Born in 1913 in Oakville, Alabama he died in 1980, while the USA Track and Field's highest accolade, the Jesse Owens Award, is named in his honour.

In the world of music, **Mark Owen**, born in 1972 in Oldham, Lancashire is the English singer and songwriter best known as a member, along with Gary Barlow, Robbie Williams, Jason Orange and Howard Donald, of the band Take That, first formed in 1989.

Internationally best-selling albums include the debut 1992 *Take That & Party*, *Everything Changes* and *Nobody*, while Owen has also enjoyed a highly successful solo career.

From music to the equally creative world of the written word, **Daniel Owen** was the distinguished writer recognised as the foremost Welsh wordsmith of the nineteenth century.

Born in 1836 in Mold, Flintshire his family was plunged into abject poverty when his father and two older brothers were killed in a mining accident less than a year after he was born.

Not receiving any formal education apart from what he learned at his local church Sunday school, he was apprenticed as a tailor when aged 12.

Later describing this apprenticeship as "a kind of a college" because the tailor shop was also a forum for discussion on a wide range of topics between customers and fellow employees, he began writing poetry and novels.

Writing verse under the nom-de-plume *Glaslwyn* he also penned the 1885 *Rhys Lewis*, recognised as the first novel written in Welsh.

Other major works include his 1891 *Gwen Tomas* and, in the same year as his death in 1895, the short story collection *Straeon y Pentan*.

Commemorated by a statue in his home town of Mold, the Daniel Owen Memorial Prize is awarded at the annual Welsh curtural event known as the National Eisteddfod for the best unpublished novel of not less than 50,000 words.

One bearer of the proud name of Owen with a rather unusual claim to fame was the English biologist, comparative anatomist and palaeontologist **Sir Richard Owen** – responsible for coining the term "Dinosauria", meaning "Fearfully Great Reptile" or "Terrible Reptile."

Born in Lancaster in 1804, the son of a wealthy merchant, he was apprenticed as an apothecary when aged 16 while he later studied medicine at Edinburgh University.

Appointed Hunterian professor in the Royal

College of Medicine in 1830, it was while later serving as superintendent of what was then the natural history department of the British Museum that he coined the term "Dinosauri" after examining the skeletons of creatures that had roamed the earth many millions of years ago.

Recognised as the driving force behind the establishment in 1881 of what is now the Natural History Museum, London and the recipient of a knighthood, he died in 1892.